C000140783

Lancaster Castle

A BRIEF HISTORY

John Champness

Lancashire Books Ltd
2014

LANCASTER CASTLE
A Brief History

By John Champness

Published by Lancashire Books Ltd, 2014

First published by Lancaster County Books, 1993
in conjunction with the Lancaster Castle Project and
Lancashire County Council Property Services

Acknowledgements;
To write even this brief history would have been
impossible without the co-operation of many people,
and I wish to acknowledge the help and advice given
by colleagues in Bedfordshire County Record Office,
The Duchy of Lancaster, H.M. Prison Service,
Lancaster County Library and Museums Department
And Lancashire Record Office, Lancaster Castle
Project Team, Lancaster Tourism, Lancaster
University. The Lord Chancellor's Office, and the
Musée des Beaux-Arts at Rouen. I am especially
grateful to colleagues in the County Planning
Department – to the typists who made sense of my
manuscripts and to Maria Rogers, who painted the
Bird's-eye View – and no less to Andrew White, the
Curator of the Lancaster City Museums, who has
always been willing to discuss information and suggest
illustrations. JC.

Welcome to Lancaster Castle

STANDING PROUDLY ON ITS HILLTOP, with its battlemented walls and towers silhouetted against the sky, Lancaster Castle is the finest historic monument in the North West of England. Not merely are its medieval and Georgian buildings, which dominate most views of the town, of considerable architectural quality, but its site is also of great significance to Lancashire's social and economic history.

For seven centuries after 1182 this was the headquarters of the County's local government, first under the Sheriffs and, later, under the Justices of the Peace in Quarter Sessions. For even longer it was the centre for the administration of justice in the County Palatine of Lancaster: more than half of the site is still occupied by one of Her Majesty's prisons, and much of the rest is still in use as a court of law.

Lancaster Castle has, however, more than local significance: it is in the ownership of Her Majesty the Queen, in right of her Duchy of Lancaster. Viewed alongside the neighbouring Priory Church, which was founded in 1094—within a year of the building of the first Castle—it symbolises the close co-operation between Church and State which underlies so much of English history.

It is proposed that the law courts will soon be transferred to Preston, and that the prison will close within the next few years. When that happens, the massive doors in John of Gaunt's Gatehouse will open to reveal the large central courtyard and its surrounding buildings. Until then much of the Castle's history can be glimpsed by walking around outside the walls, and a flavour of the lives of some of the former inhabitants can be discovered by a visit to those parts of the interior which are open to the public. This beautifully illustrated brief history of the Castle will, I hope, encourage you to visit this, the County's premier historic building.

The Rt Hon The Earl of Derby
Constable of the Castle

Lancaster Castle and the Priory Church in the 1840s, seen from Cable Street. (Lancaster City Museums)

The Norman Fortress

LANCASTER CASTLE has dominated the town for 900 years, ever since it was first established in 1093, but the hill on which it stands has a history which goes back a thousand years further. As the Romans pushed the frontier of their Empire up the north west side of Britain, the Governor of the Province, Agricola, built a fort here in AD 79 to control the lowest crossing point of the River Lune. There are remains of this and at least two other successive Roman forts beneath the surface of Castle Hill, but little is known of them, and the unbroken history of the site and its visible buildings starts at the end of the eleventh century.

At that time there was no Lancashire. The areas which we call the Lake District and Lancashire north of the River Ribble were then an outlying part of the Earldom of Northumbria and thus a sort of no man's land, claimed by the Kings both of England and Scotland. In 1092, however, the English King William Rufus settled the question once and for all by capturing Carlisle, and fixing the northern border of England along a line which has remained unchanged to this day. In this campaign William had been helped by his kinsman, Roger of Poitou, who held lands south of the Ribble, and, in gratitude for his support, the King doubled the area of his estates. Henceforth Roger held all the lands west of the Pennines between the Mersey and the southern fringes of the Lake District beyond Morecambe Bay, and in time these lands became known as the Honour of Lancaster. In return, he swore to be loyal to the King and was responsible to him for the defence of these areas against possible attacks by Scottish armies.

Before the Norman Conquest the Lancaster area had been administered from Halton, five kilometres up the Lune Valley, but Roger had wider responsibilities. In 1093 therefore he established his military headquarters here in Lancaster on the site of the Roman fort. Like the Romans he needed to control the river crossing, but he also needed to see the other side of Morecambe Bay, for in those days the main road from Scotland ran not over Shap Fell but around the Cumbrian coast. In the following year, 1094, as many other Norman barons had done, he founded a small Benedictine monastery on the site of the present Priory Church—as a thank-offering for his worldly success and also, perhaps, in the hope of divine protection.

No trace of Roger's stronghold survives above ground, but it is hoped that, before too long, excavations behind the present Castle walls may reveal its plan, its size and something of how its garrison lived. It was probably no more than a simple oval-shaped enclosure, fortified by a timber palisade; it may possibly have been built with an earthen mound as well, crowned with a timber stockade, as was the nearby 'castle' at Halton. Such a relatively simple fortress could have been built by forced labour in a matter of days rather than months and would have been large enough to accommodate a small garrison of men-at-arms and mounted knights. It used to be thought that Roger of Poitou built the great Keep of the Castle, but its size and shape suggest to modern scholars that this is most unlikely.

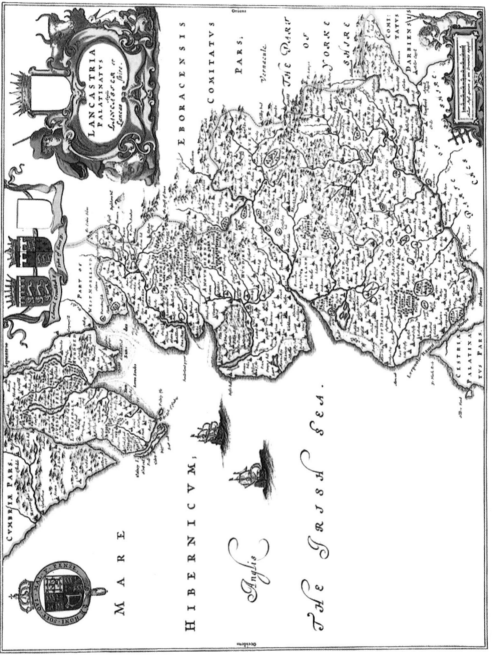

Blaeu's Map of the County Palatine, published in 1645, shows how Roger of Poitou's landholdings, originally south of the Ribble, were extended northwards and across Morecambe Bay to form what became the Honour of Lancaster. (Lancashire County Library)

The Honour of Lancaster

ROGER OF POITOU was Lord of the Honour of Lancaster for less than ten years. After the death of William Rufus in 1100, many Norman barons believed that William the Conqueror's eldest son, Robert the Duke of Normandy, should become the next King of England, rather than his fourth son who was in fact crowned as Henry I. Roger joined this rebellion, but it was unsuccessful, and so the Honour of Lancaster was confiscated from him by the King in 1102.

Thereafter the history of the Honour is complicated. Very briefly, Henry I granted it to his nephew Stephen of Blois, who was crowned King in 1135. Henry's daughter, Matilda, then rebelled against King Stephen and great disorder followed. However, Stephen bought peace and quiet on his northern frontier in 1141 by allowing David, King of Scotland, to occupy the Honour of Lancaster as far south as the Ribble. Matilda's rebellion came to an end in 1153 with a general agreement whereby, when Stephen died, Matilda's son, Henry Plantagenet, should succeed to the English throne (as Henry II). The Honour of Lancaster was to be held by Stephen's son, William, and not by the King of Scotland. Later, when William died in 1164, the Honour was brought back under the direct control of Henry II and was treated as a normal county, administered by a Sheriff in the name of the King.

The County of Lancaster was first mentioned by name in 1168 but does not appear to have been administered separately from Northumbria until 1182.

This extract from Robert Freebairn's watercolour (on page 12) shows the Keep with its original entrance on the first floor, now hidden by the Debtors' Wing of 1796.
(Lancaster City Museums)

Thomas Hearne's watercolour, painted around 1778, shows the west side of the Keep before the building of the Crown Court. The round tower just to the right was demolished in 1796 to make way for the Shire Hall, but the wall beyond this still exists, as does Adrian's Tower at the very end. (Lancaster City Museums)

It was probably during these troubled times in the mid-twelfth century that the great stone Keep (1)* was built. Its purpose was to provide accommodation for the Castle's lord (or his resident deputy, the Constable) and—if the Castle were ever besieged—a refuge of last resort for the garrison. Nobody knows, however, when this building work was done or who paid for it.

The Keep is a four-storey tower, 20 metres high and with a shallow buttress at each corner and halfway along each side. Its outer walls are about 3 metres thick, and it is divided internally by a central wall into two rooms on each floor.

The original entrance was on the first floor of the south side, at the head of a flight of stone steps, and could still be seen in the late eighteenth century, before the County Gaol was extended. Building such a tower in stone

was in the twelfth century (and would be now) a long and labour-intensive process, involving a small army of skilled craftsmen and labourers to cut and lay the stone and build in wood the necessary scaffolding, floors, doors and roofs.

The Keep would have taken at least five years to build and cost at least £1,000 in the money of the day, but no mention of such sums or of its construction (as distinct from repairs to it) has been found in the royal account books. However, these are far from complete for the Lancashire area in the twelfth century, and the intriguing suggestion has been made that the Keep was built by King David I of Scotland while he controlled Cumbria and North Lancashire. For the moment this must be no more than speculation, but in any case the Castle was firmly in the hands of Henry II by 1164.

The arms of the Borough of Lancaster have traditionally comprised a fleur-de-lys above a lion. This seal, which is thought to date from 1432, is, however, dominated by what must be the earliest surviving image of the Castle. (Lancaster City Museums)

---

* Figures in brackets after the name of a part of the Castle refer to the bird's eye view on the centre pages.

Walls and Towers

ON THE DEATH OF Henry II in 1189, the Crown was inherited by his eldest son Richard I, who then granted the Honour of Lancaster to his younger brother John, in the vain hope that this would guarantee his loyalty. When John himself became King in 1199, he knew the risks of losing control of the Honour of Lancaster, and so it remained in royal hands through all of his troubled reign and most of that of his son, Henry III.

For perhaps a generation, Henry II's Castle at Lancaster, with its stone Keep surrounded by a timber stockade, was as up-to-date as most in the kingdom, but towards the end of the twelfth century—thanks to the experience gained during the Crusades—the techniques of siege warfare advanced. Mechanical catapults could hurl large stones with great force and accuracy, and the skills of undermining walls were improved. Consequently, it became increasingly important to strengthen the outer defences of a castle and, in the course of time, timber palisades were replaced by curtain walls of stone. These were strengthened at intervals by stone towers which projected in front of them, so that defenders could shoot arrows from the side at anyone approaching the base of the walls.

The royal accounts from the reign of King John show that considerable sums—more than £630—were spent, mostly between 1209 and 1211, on building works at the Castle. These included digging a ditch on the south and west sides, and also work on 'the King's lodgings'. This presumably involved the building of Adrian's Tower (2), the round tower in the south-west corner of the present Castle. (It is so called because people used to think that it was built in the time of the Roman Emperor, Hadrian, but its masonry dates, beyond reasonable doubt, to the early thirteenth century.) This medieval masonry can be seen inside the Tower, but the outside was refaced at the end of the eighteenth century, as part of the remodelling of the Shire Hall and Crown Court (see page 29).

Further references in the royal accounts of Henry III's reign to the spending of nearly £200 in 1243 on repairs to the Keep and on works on the Gatehouse and palisades, and over £250 in 1254 on curtain walls and the gateway, suggest that soon after the middle of the thirteenth century the Keep was surrounded by a ring of walls with occasional towers. A square medieval tower, called the Dungeon Tower—like the still existing Well Tower—used to stand between the Gatehouse and Adrian's Tower until it was demolished in 1818, and evidence of another round tower was discovered in the mid-1790s when the Male Felons' Prison was built.

For about 150 years from the middle of the thirteenth century there are no mentions in the surviving royal accounts of significant building work at Lancaster Castle; but these accounts are in fact not complete, so it may well be that work was done, though no records of it remain. The still extant Well Tower (3), for example, whose basement contains two of the Castle's many wells and also three vaulted, stone-flagged underground storerooms (which may have been used to accommodate prisoners) is thought to have been largely built in the early fourteenth century. If no more significant building work took place, it is probably because the strategic situation of the Castle did not justify any more expense than was necessary for repairs and maintenance. Lancaster was not near a frontier, and, apart from short-lived Scottish invasions in 1322 and 1389—which did in fact cause damage to the Castle—there was nearly always relative peace on the English side of the Border. Furthermore, although the Earldom and, later, the

This drawing—probably the earliest illustration of the Castle—was made in 1562 as part of a survey of Duchy castles in the North of England. It shows the Gatehouse and the Keep clearly, with the Well Tower to the right in front, and what must be Adrian's Tower to the left. (P.R.O., DL 31/112)

Duchy (see page 43), bore the name of Lancaster and included many parts of Lancashire, more of the landholdings lay outside rather than within Lancashire; and so, provided that there were no major problems in Lancaster, it was regarded as somewhat marginal.

This view of the inner courtyard looking towards the Gatehouse—the first of the watercolours by Robert Freebairn reproduced in this book—was painted in 1800 from an earlier drawing, but appears to be accurate. As well as the Gatehouse it shows, from right to left, the Dungeon Tower (demolished in 1818), the Well Tower, and the Bowling Green (shown on Mackreth's map on page 23). (Lancaster City Museums)

John of Gaunt's Gatehouse

THIS SITUATION CHANGED, however, after 1399 when Henry, Duke of Lancaster, became King Henry IV of England (see page 44). Almost immediately he began to build the present imposing Gatehouse (4) at considerable expense. He had sound military reasons for doing this since the Castle had been damaged and the area had been devastated during the Scottish invasion in 1389; a similar attack would have been a public humiliation for a King who was also the Duke of Lancaster. By about 1400 the gateway to the Castle, which had been built in the reign of John or Henry III and was probably no more than an arch between two round towers with outer defences of timber, would have been old-fashioned and inadequate to cope with a full-scale attack by a contemporary army. The decision was therefore taken to make the new Gatehouse as strong and as impressive as possible, and it probably replaced the Keep as the strongest part of the Castle. It not only served as a warning to possible attackers, but also as an ostentatious symbol of Henry's kingly power in the town from which his Duchy took its name.

This statue of John of Gaunt was placed in a canopied niche which originally contained the statue of a saint. The shields still show traces of the original carving of the royal coat of arms. (Lancaster Castle Project)

Although the Keep is the biggest medieval building in the Castle, the Gatehouse is the most impressive. Indeed, with its sturdy, semi-octagonal towers rising 20 metres above their massive sloping plinths, its portcullis and its battlements built out over corbels (so that missiles could be dropped on anyone trying to break down the gates), it is perhaps the finest of its date and type in England.

It was traditionally believed to have been built for John of Gaunt, and a statue of him was placed in the niche above the Gateway in 1822 to confirm the tradition, but the truth is more interesting than the fiction. The evidence for the traditional belief was that on either side of the niche is a shield carved with the arms of the Kings of England (three leopards) quartered with those of the Kings of France (three fleurs-de-lys)—because the Kings of England also claimed to be Kings of France. The right-hand shield bears in addition a sign rather like a wide 'm' which is called a label and in heraldry denotes the son and heir of the person whose shield is on the left-hand side. A bit of wishful thinking

Edward Buckler's engraving of 1864 shows John of Gaunt's Gatehouse, with the Gaoler's House just beyond. The railings were placed around the Castle ditch in 1825. Only the piers now remain. (Lancaster City Museums)

£133) per year on building work at Lancaster Castle and that, between 1402 and 1422 (when Henry V died) more than £2,500 was spent here. This was more than enough to build the Gatehouse, and substantial work may well have been carried out to modify the top storey of the Keep (which has thinner walls than the lower storeys) and perhaps also the Well Tower.

On each of its two upper floors, the Gatehouse has three rooms; the apartment on the first floor was probably used by the Constable of the Castle before the Civil War. After then most of the Gatehouse rooms were occupied by debtors (see page 37) and one of the most attractive pictures of the Castle courtyard (see page 26) was drawn from the window of one of these rooms.

Once completed with its strengthened Gatehouse, Keep and curtain walls, the Castle—fortunately for the people of Lancaster—saw no significant military action for nearly 250 years. A survey in 1578 led to extensive repairs to the Keep and its roof (at a cost of some £235), and the fortifications were strengthened in 1585 in case there should be a Spanish invasion. It is just possible to see a stone in the centre of the northern battlements which bears the initials ER RA and the date 1585, and this must commemorate the works carried out in that year for Queen Elizabeth by her Sheriff, Richard Assheton. The Armada was a failure, and no shot was fired in anger at Lancaster Castle until the Civil War.

therefore linked the Gatehouse with John of Gaunt— Shakespeare's 'time-honoured Lancaster'—for he was a son of King Edward III.

It is now known, however, that the arms of the King of France were not changed to three fleurs-de-lys until 1403, so the Gatehouse must have been finished after then. Furthermore, the first King of England after that date who had a son and heir was Henry IV, who ruled between 1399 and 1413. The heraldic evidence is confirmed by the royal accounts which show that, after 1402, the Duchy staff were authorised to spend 200 marks (a little over

The Castle in the Civil War

LANCASTER CASTLE has belonged to the reigning monarch from 1399 until today, so at first sight it is surprising that it was not properly garrisoned when hostilities started at the end of 1642. King Charles I's main concern was, however, to capture London, and he relied on the local gentry (who were largely Royalist) to keep control of their counties. In Lancashire they underestimated the support in most towns for Parliament, and Lancaster Castle fell to a small army sent from Preston in February 1643. A Parliamentary garrison was installed, and defensive earthworks were thrown up at the entries to the town. These were stormed by Royalist troops in March 1643, but a siege of the Castle was called off after two days, when the news came that a relief army was setting out from Preston. Two further, somewhat half-hearted attempts by Royalist armies to recapture the Castle took place in April and June 1643 but did not succeed, and after that all four towns on Lancashire's main north–south road—Lancaster, Preston, Wigan and Warrington—were in Parliamentary hands until the war ended a year or so later.

Thereafter the days of the Castle's military importance appeared to be numbered. In 1645 orders were given that 'all the walls about it should be thrown down' with 'only the gatehouse, the buildings upon the south and west with towers' being retained. These orders, and a subsequent command in March 1647 at the end of the first Civil War, that the new defensive works should be removed after the garrison had been withdrawn, were probably not carried out since a Parliamentary garrison, hurriedly placed there when the Scots under the Duke of Hamilton marched south in support of Charles I, was able to withstand a short siege by a Royalist army in August 1648.

After the execution of Charles I in January 1649, Parliament gave orders again that the Castle should be demolished 'except such parts there as are necessary for the sitting of the

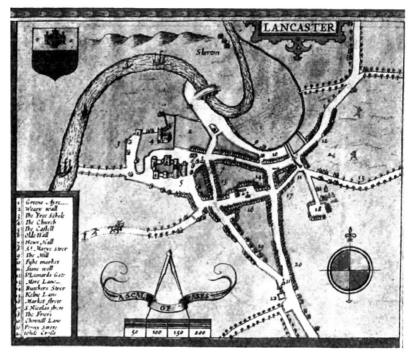

John Speed's map of the County Palatine, published in 1610, gives the earliest plan of Lancaster and, again, shows a castle in the Borough's coat of arms. The Castle and the Priory Church clearly stood on the edge of the town, and this was still true when Freebairn made his paintings in 1800. (Lancashire County Library)

This Freebairn watercolour is the companion to the one on page 8 and shows the courtyard from the Gatehouse, before the rebuilding works of the 1790s—with the Dungeon Tower on the left and the Keep on the right. Freebairn never saw this view and copied it from unclear earlier drawings, which he had difficulty in interpreting. The medieval Hall of the Castle is in the background; it looks as though it was approached up a staircase on the left, but it is not obvious how this was built or where it led.

(Lancaster City Museums)

This view of the Castle and Priory Church, perched on their hill above the river, was published in 1728 by Samuel and Nathaniel Buck, and became a classic image of the town. It seems to show that, after the Civil War, there was no curtain wall between the Gatehouse and the Well Tower to its right. (Lancaster City Museums)

Courts of justice and for the keepe of the common gaol of the County'. The Governor of the Castle seems to have been reluctant to carry out these orders, for the Castle was still defensible in March 1651. When, on 12 August of that year, the young Charles II was proclaimed King as he passed through Lancaster (at the head of an army which was to be defeated at Worcester on 3 September), he had the Castle gates opened and all the prisoners released.

After Charles' restoration to the throne in 1660, the High Sheriff and Justices of the Peace of the County sent him a petition, asking that the Castle be 'repaired as formerly', with 'several strong and stately towers and lines' (that is to say, curtain walls) since the latter had been 'demolished in the late unhappy wars, and the roof of the towers and lodgings of the officers are fallen into decay, and the records [are] in danger of

spoil'. A survey of the fabric and of 'all the decays and ruins thereof' was carried out in December 1663, and an estimate of £1,957 was given for the cost of the works considered necessary. These involved repairs to the stonework of the Keep and the Gatehouse, of the Judges' Hall and the Crown Office (south west of the Keep) and to the timber floors and roofs in the kitchen and the southern half of the Keep. The northern half of the Keep was left a roofless shell, but the southern half was kept in use, with the Shire Hall (or Civil Court) on the first floor (behind the big window) and a room for debtors (called the Quakers' Room) above it; the basement was used as the 'madhouse' until the County Lunatic Asylum was built in 1816. The curtain walls were probably not repaired, since no attempt was made to defend the Castle against the Jacobite forces in 1715.

The Castle as a
Court of Law and Prison

ONCE THE CASTLE had no military value—
and the drawing published by the Buck
brothers in 1728 (see page 13) does suggest that
the wall between the Gatehouse and the Well
Tower had been demolished—its significance
in what one might call the maintenance of law
and order in Lancashire was no longer over-
shadowed by military matters.

The Parliamentary Order in 1649 that the
demolition of the Castle should not include
the buildings necessary for the County Gaol
and Courts of Justice was by no means the
first mention of these functions at Lancaster
Castle. The first reference to a gaol in the
Castle goes back to 1196 and was brief; other,
later ones were often more elo-
quent. A survey of the buildings
carried out for Queen Elizabeth's
government in 1562, for example,
mentioned 'the Gaol and
Sessions there kept' and regarded
the Castle as 'a great strength to
the Country and succour to the
Queen's Justices'. Incidentally,
we owe to this survey the first
illustration of the Castle (see
page 7).

Ever since the twelfth century
in Lancashire (and from well
before that in most other parts
of the country) the King had
nominated a major local land-
owner to be the Sheriff (that is,
his deputy) in the County. The
Sheriff of Lancaster, whose office
was in the Castle, was responsible to the King not only for
the collection of the taxes due to
the Crown, but also for the
preservation of the 'King's

Peace'—by calling out the militia whenever
necessary and by organising the Assizes, that
is the law courts where serious criminal cases
could be tried twice a year. (The first Assizes
in Lancaster were held in 1166.) The Earls
and Dukes of Lancaster were automatically
Sheriffs of the County (though they did appoint
deputies); and even when the Dukes achieved
palatine powers (see page 43), they were still
responsible to the King for the organisation
of the Assizes and for the appointment of the
judges who would try both the civil and criminal cases. The Duchy Council, created by
Henry IV, retained its responsibility for the
law courts in Lancashire until 1873.

The reverse of the seal of the Duchy of Lancaster, made in 1830 for
William IV. (Lancaster Castle Project)

Some Early Trials

THE COURTS of the Earls and Dukes of Lancaster must have been held in the hall of the medieval Castle. This was a largish building (about 15 metres long by 8 metres wide) which stood on the site of the present Barristers' Library and Robing Room, to the south of the present Crown Court. Its basement remains—the so-called Dungeons which one can visit after Adrian's Tower—but most of the rest was demolished or hidden by new masonry at the end of the eighteenth century; we only know of its appearance from a few unclear drawings of that period. It was, however, the scene of a number of notorious trials whose records survive. One which has become a part of Lancashire's folklore was the trial of the so-called 'Pendle Witches' in 1612.

While we accept nowadays that, in an age before medicine had a scientific basis, people had recourse to 'wise women' for potions and spells to heal the sick, we find it difficult to believe that magic and curses can cause harm. Four centuries ago, however, many people, including King James I, did believe in witchcraft, and an Act of Parliament was passed in 1604. This defined it as 'making a covenant with an evil spirit, using a corpse for magic, hurting life or limb, procuring love or injuring cattle by means of charms'; it also imposed the death penalty on those found guilty.

Behind the story of the Pendle Witches lies an incident near Colne on 18 March 1612. A pedlar from Halifax refused to give some pins to a beggar, Alizon Device. She was angry with him, and he had a stroke almost immediately afterwards. The pedlar's son accused

THE
WONDERFVLL
DISCOVERIE OF
WITCHES IN THE COVN-
TIE OF LAN-
CASTER.

With the Arraignement and Triall of Nineteene notorious WITCHES, at the Aſſizes and generall Gaole deliuerie, holden at the Caſtle of LANCASTER, vpon *Munday*, the seuenteenth of *Auguſt* laſt, 1612.

Before Sir IAMES ALTHAM, and Sir EDWARD BROMLEY, Knights; BARONS of his Maieſties Court of EXCHEQVER: And Iuſtices of *Aſſize*, Oyer and Terminor, *and generall* Gaole deliuerie in the circuit of the *North Parts*.

Together with the Arraignement and Triall of IENNET PRESTON, *at the Aſſizes holden at the Caſtle of Yorke, the seuen and twentieth day of Iulie laſt paſt,* with her Execution for the murther of Maſter LISTER *by Witchcraft*.

Publiſhed and ſet forth by commandement of his Maieſties Iuſtices of Aſſize in the North Parts.

By THOMAS POTTS Eſquier.

LONDON,
Printed by *W. Stansby* for *Iohn Barnes,* dwelling neare Holborne Conduit. 1613.

The title page of Thomas Potts' best-selling account of the trial of the 'Pendle Witches'. (Lancashire County Library)

This Freebairn watercolour is the counterpart of the one on page 8 and shows some of the new buildings, designed by Thomas Harrison—the Gaoler's House to the left of the Gatehouse, and the Female Felons' Prison on the right. On the far left is the wall separating the Male Felons' Prison from the courtyard, which was reserved for debtors.

(Lancaster City Museums)

her of witchcraft, and the investigations in April by the local magistrate, Roger Nowell of Read Hall, brought forth a tangled web of accusations and counter-accusations between the members of three local families. Most magistrates would have let the matter rest there, inconclusively. However, a few days later, Nowell was told of a meeting on Good Friday at which, it was said, a number of 'witches' had conspired to blow up Lancaster Castle and to murder Thomas Covell the Keeper. (He lived in the house now called the Judges' Lodgings.) Since Nowell had been the High Sheriff in 1610, he felt obliged, only a few years after the Gunpowder Plot, to send the 'witches' for trial and he was in fact the prosecutor. His chief witness was the nine-year-old sister of Alizon Device! In the event, the judges found ten of the defendants, eight women and two men, guilty—of witchcraft, not conspiracy—and on 20 August 1612, the day after the trial ended, they were hanged on Lancaster Moor. A local tradition says that they were kept during their trial in the basement of the Well Tower, and for this reason the tower is sometimes called the Witches' Tower.

Other probable miscarriages of justice concern people whom we would today consider as prisoners of conscience—mostly Roman Catholics and Quakers. Again, it is difficult for us who live in a fairly sceptical, fairly tolerant age to think ourselves back into the minds of many of our ancestors, who did not regard disagreements with the Church of England on religious matters as merely personal concerns, but saw them as expressions of opposition to the political powers that be. The western half of Lancashire in Elizabethan times was an area where many people (including several gentry families) remained loyal to the 'old faith' of Roman Catholicism. Many were forced to pay fines for not attending church, and a few suffered imprisonment, but that was all.

However, after 1570 when the Pope excommunicated Queen Elizabeth and thereby encouraged her assassination, Roman Catholic priests were regarded by the Queen's ministers as the Pope's fifth column, enemies of Protestant England and automatically guilty of high treason. Those who were caught in Lancashire were brought to trial at Lancaster and inevitable punishment— the deliberately horrendous and humiliating public death by hanging, drawing and quartering. Eleven priests—the most famous being Edmund Arrowsmith— but also four laymen met their death in this way on Lancaster Moor, between 1583 and 1646; some are now counted among the English Martyrs who were beatified by the Pope in 1987.

After the Restoration a number of early Quakers, including their leader George Fox, were imprisoned in Lancaster Castle. It was not so much their stinging criticisms of the Church of England which led them to gaol. They were regarded as politically suspect— Fox was accused of being 'a disturber of the peace of the nation'—because they treated all men, and women, as equals in the eyes of God and also refused to confirm their loyalty to Charles II by swearing an oath. Some of them died in prison, but none was executed.

South View of Lancaster CASTLE.

The Arms of JOHN of GAUNT Duke of LANCASTER on the Gate Tower.

This attractive engraving appears on Stephen Mackreth's map of Lancaster, published in 1778; it shows—more clearly than the Buck engraving on page 13—the medieval Castle as it had survived the Civil War and before it was changed in the 1790s. From right to left one can see the Well Tower, the Gatehouse, the Keep, the now-demolished Dungeon Tower, and Adrian's Tower, which was encased in Georgian Gothic stonework in 1798. (Lancashire County Library)

The Work of the JPs

IN HIS WORK of maintaining law and order the Sheriff was helped, from the late thirteenth century and perhaps earlier, by a handful of middling landowners who were first called Keepers of the Peace and, after 1361, Justices of the Peace. In that year an Act of Parliament gave them the power to act as magistrates and try minor criminal offences; a further Act in 1363 laid down that they should meet in sessions four times per year, at Easter, Midsummer, Michaelmas (late September) and Epiphany (early January). After the Wars of the Roses, Henry VII and the other Tudor monarchs increased both the number of JPs and also their responsibilities in an attempt to reduce the power of major landholders. By the end of Elizabeth's reign there were about three dozen JPs in each county and they had replaced the Sheriffs in the administration of local affairs.

By the time of Charles II the Duchy Council in London not only organised the Assizes, but also nominated the JPs—as it still does—and supervised their work in the Quarter Sessions. Because of the great extent of the traditional County Palatine the JPs normally met first at Lancaster Castle and then 'adjourned' to other meetings at more convenient centres like Preston, Wigan or Manchester. They were advised on matters of law and detailed administrative procedure by a legal officer, called the Clerk of the Peace, who kept records of their meetings. In 1663 the office of Clerk was obtained by a lawyer called Roger Kenyon, and it remained in his family for several generations. He is the first Clerk of the Peace of whom a portrait exists, and a copy of his likeness can be seen in the Grand Jury

Room in the background of the portrait of Sir Patrick McCall, who was the last Clerk of the Peace when the Quarter Sessions were abolished in 1971.

The Justices in Quarter Sessions continued to act as magistrates until 1971, but they also served as the local authority for the whole of Lancashire until 1889, when the elected County Council met for the first time. Many of their duties involved supervising the work of parish officers—such as Constables and Overseers of the Poor, and of the roads—but they were also concerned in the organisation of the County Gaol, though this was still the nominal responsibility of the Sheriff.

The portrait in the Grand Jury Room of Sir Patrick McCall and his predecessor, Roger Kenyon. (Lancaster Castle Project)

Lancaster

9. *Shire Hall*
1798

2. *Adrian's Tower*
c. 1210

10. *Female*
Penitentiary
1821

8. *Debtors' Wing*
1796

6. *Female Felons'*
Prison, 1793

4. *John of Gaunt's*
Gatehouse
c. 1400

In 1877 the County Gaol in Lancaster Castle became no more than one of Her Majesty's Prisons. This bird's-eye view by Maria Rogers gives an idea of its layout and appearance in that significant year. (Lancaster Castle Project)

1. *Keep*
   c. 1150

7. *Male Felons'*
   Prison, 1796

3. *Well Tower*
   c. 1325

5. *Gaoler's House*
   1788

Life in the County Gaol

IFE IN EIGHTEENTH-CENTURY GAOLS was generally somewhat disorganised, and Lancaster Castle was no exception. The reason lay not so much in the shortcomings of individuals, as in the way that the role of prisons had been expanded, without much thought, in response to changing pressures. County Gaols had originally been intended to provide short-term, secure accommodation for people awaiting trial at the Assizes, or for convicted criminals who were waiting for their sentences to be carried out—by hanging, by transfer to a 'house of correction' (which corresponded roughly to our modern idea of a prison) or, later, by transportation to an overseas colony.

In the course of the seventeenth century these people had been joined by debtors (who were normally free men and women who could avoid formal bankruptcy by forfeiting their freedom until their

A contemporary portrait of John Howard.
(Bedfordshire County Record Office)

finances improved). During the eighteenth century numbers were again increased by a third group—long-stay 'felons', that is, convicted criminals who had not been sentenced to death but could not, for various reasons, be transported or accommodated in a house of correction. County Gaols were therefore often overcrowded, but perhaps the worst feature of Georgian gaols was that little attempt was made to separate prisoners according to their category; debtors were mixed up with convicted criminals and with people on remand awaiting trial.

The County Gaol, in Lancashire as elsewhere, was nominally under the control of the High Sheriff, but he was in office for no more than a year and could therefore do little to improve conditions, even if he wanted to and knew what to do. Complaints could be made by prisoners to the Assize judges, and these normally resulted in small improvements, for example to leaking roofs or smoking fires. In most years during the eighteenth century about £100 was spent on repairs and improvements at the Castle, but no major changes took place until the 1780s. The Justices of the Peace had the right to inspect the County Gaol and were generally humane squires, but they too had few ideas about what should be done and not enough time to study the problems and discuss the solutions. Little progress was therefore made until an exceptional man had done just this.

This man was John Howard (1726–90), a Bedfordshire squire and JP. In 1773, as High Sheriff, he was shocked by the physical conditions which he found in Bedford Gaol, but even more so by the injustice of a system which forced a prisoner, who had spent some

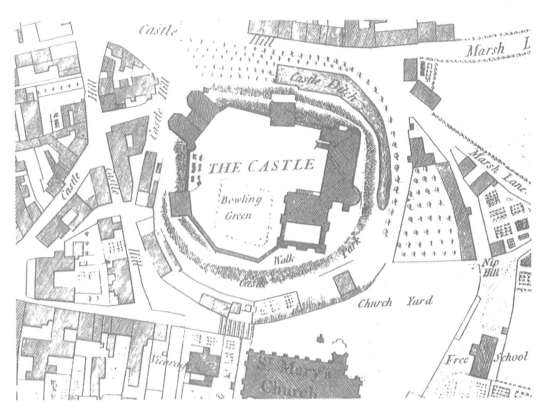

Mackreth's map of Lancaster was drawn, probably for aesthetic reasons, with north at the bottom of the sheet, with
the result that the Castle appears upside down to 20th-century eyes—with the Gatehouse in the 'north-west' corner of
the courtyard. Reading clockwise from the Gatehouse one sees the square Dungeon Tower, the round Adrian's Tower
at the south end of the medieval Hall, the round tower (which appears in Hearne's watercolour on page 4), the Keep—
of which the northern half has no roof—and the Well Tower. The present curtain wall around the Male Felons' Prison
runs through what were in 1778 the gardens of houses on the south side of the churchyard.
(Lancashire County Library)

time in the gaol and had been acquitted at his
trial, to return to gaol until he had paid the
fees demanded by the Keeper. Howard then
suggested to the Bedfordshire JPs that the
Keeper should be paid a salary, rather than
rely for his living on these fees and other
'perks'. Though sympathetic to the idea, they
wanted to know if any other County paid its
Keeper a salary, before they would accept
Howard's suggestion. So he visited sixteen
gaols in neighbouring counties and found that
things were just as bad.

In 1774, under pressure from John Howard
and those whom he had persuaded of the
good sense of his proposals, Parliament
passed two Acts which laid down that
Keepers could be paid salaries, that remand

prisoners found not guilty must be freed in
open court, that prisoners should be sepa-
rated according to their sex and their category, that they should have communal day
rooms but single cells for sleeping, and that
sanitation and ventilation should be improved
in the hope of reducing 'gaol fever' (now
called typhus). This was of great concern to
contemporary JPs, since gaol fever killed
more people (including gaolers) in a year than
were hanged. (It was believed that the illness
was transmitted through stale, damp air; it is
now known that it is passed on by the bites of
body lice.)

Howard had these two Acts printed and
sent at his expense to all the Keepers in
England. Thereafter he spent several months

This Freebairn watercolour is the counterpart of the one on page 12 and shows the Debtors' Wing to the left of the Keep and, to the right, the Male Felons' Prison with its two towers and, in front of them, the two-storey Turnkey's Lodge. (Lancaster City Museums)

These so-called Dungeons, which in their present form probably date from the 18th century rather than the Middle Ages, are in the basement of the medieval Hall next to Adrian's Tower. (Lancaster Castle Project)

each year until he died—of gaol fever in Russia—travelling the length and breadth of Europe, visiting and revisiting prisons to encourage every authority to adopt the standards of the best. He travelled about 100,000 kilometres—largely on horseback, because he could not stomach the smell of his clothes in a carriage after he had visited a prison—and spent at least £30,000 of his own money in fifteen years on this work—about as much as it cost to rebuild the County Gaol in Lancaster Castle in the two decades around 1800.

Howard first visited Lancaster Castle in 1776 and in his book, *The State of the Prisons*, published in the following year, he remarked on the spacious central courtyard (with its enclosed bowling green) but also on the lack of an infirmary—although sick prisoners were well treated. He described how the thirty-two debtors had several 'apartments', including one called The Oven (in Adrian's Tower) and one called The Quakers' Room (in the Keep) and how they could walk and work—at such activities as spinning and knitting—in the Crown Hall and Shire Hall when they were not in use as the criminal and civil courts. The nineteen felons had separate day rooms for men and women; at night the women slept in their dayroom, while the men slept in two vaulted cells, which were 'close, dark and noisome'—probably in the now-demolished Dungeon Tower, rather than in the Well Tower.

This pen-and-wash drawing of the courtyard, as seen from one of the debtors' rooms in the Gatehouse, was made in 1824 by James Weetman, who may have been a debtor. In addition to the buildings by Harrison (which are visible in Freebairn's watercolour on page 24) are the prison workshops in front of the Keep (probably by Harrison) and Joseph Gandy's tall Female Penitentiary, surrounded by railings, on the left. (Lancaster City Museums)

New Prisons and New Courts

THERE WERE SEVERAL Prisons Acts in the late eighteenth century, but the most important one for Lancaster Castle was the Act of 1784, which encouraged JPs to inspect County Gaols more closely and to apply for private Acts of Parliament which would allow them to re-build and enlarge County Gaols with separate accommodation for the various categories of prisoners. The Lancashire JPs had begun at the summer Assizes in August 1783 to consider such proposals and thus welcomed the Act. The organisation of Lancashire's County Gaol had already been improved along the lines which Howard advocated, and he had been pleased to notice changes between his visits in 1776 and 1779. Furthermore, in 1785, rules for the running of the Gaol were drawn up and printed; and the new Gaoler, John Higgin (the son of the Gaoler who had died of gaol fever in 1783) was persuaded to give up his 'perks' and accept an annual salary of 200 guineas (£210) paid from the county rates. Higgin was made responsible for keeping the Gaol clean and healthy, and for providing coal, bedding, soap and washing facilities for the prisoners. (One way of keeping the place clean was by regular white-washing, and in a few unfrequented places in the Well Tower successive layers of white-wash have built up to a deposit nearly a centimetre thick.)

The Lancashire JPs secured their Act of Parliament in 1788 and began to build very soon afterwards. They had already chosen their architect, Thomas Harrison, who had won the competition for the Skerton Bridge at Lancaster, which was being built at the County's expense. He had produced his first design in 1787 for separate prisons for male and female felons and for debtors. (Unfortunately, none of Harrison's plans for the Castle has survived, but what appears to be his model for the Shire Hall still exists,

although it is not yet on display.) The first building to be erected—in 1788—was the Gaoler's House (5) between the Gatehouse and the Well Tower. Like most architects of his day, Harrison preferred to design in the Classical idiom, using motifs derived from the buildings of Greece and Rome, but, since his new works were surrounded by a medieval church and by the remains of a medieval castle, he chose to use medieval motifs like battlements and Gothic windows with pointed heads, at least in the main façades.

After the Gaoler's House, work was begun in 1792 on the prison for female felons (6). This was on the other side of the Gatehouse, in a four-storey tower with Gothic windows and a canted front to the courtyard. Next, between 1794 and 1796—when a bill for painting 64 iron doors was paid—came the prison for male felons (7). This extended to the north of the Keep, well beyond the line of the medieval curtain wall, and was cut off from the outside world by the present high walls. Above these rose two and, later, three four-storey towers (again with canted fronts and Gothic windows) where the prisoners slept in separate cells—without windows. During the day, when they were not working, they could sit in one of the four day rooms or take the air in one of the four flagged courtyards which radiated from a central point where the turnkey's lodge stood; from here one gaoler could supervise them and visitors could see them without being seen.

At the same time, to the south of the Keep, two storeys of accommodation were built for debtors above an attractive open arcade with Gothic arches (8), where they could shelter in poor weather. Otherwise, they were free to spend their time in their rooms, which were also scattered around the older parts of the Castle, or to promenade around the courtyard.

Freebairn's watercolour of the extended Castle from the west shows one of the towers of the Male Felons' Prison on the left and the Shire Hall in the centre, behind the great terrace. This was probably designed as a belvedere for the fine view across Morecambe Bay to the Lakeland hills. Hanging Corner was just behind the round tower on the left of the Shire Hall—and thus well visible from the slightly raised churchyard. (Lancaster City Museums)

In 1796 the medieval Hall of the Castle, which stood to the south-west of the Keep and housed the Crown Court, was taken down; its basement survives, however, and can be visited along with Adrian's Tower. Thereafter a new Crown Court and Shire Hall (which had been in the Keep) were begun to the designs of Thomas Harrison. These form a symmetrical group to the west of the Keep, with the roughly semi-circular Shire Hall (9) projecting on to a wide terrace between the refaced Adrian's Tower on the south and a new round tower on the north.

Work now progressed more slowly, in part because money was not so readily available for major projects after the outbreak of war with France, but in part also because Harrison had, unbeknown to the JPs, moved in 1795 to Chester (where he was involved in designing the Shire Hall and Courts in Chester Castle, this time in the Classical idiom). The shell of the Crown Court was finished first, because it is a smaller, simpler building, constructed against the west wall of the Keep, but the structure of the much bigger, more complicated Shire Hall was not completed until July 1798. This delay was too great for the patience of the JPs, and Harrison was asked to resign. He was probably relieved to do so. The JPs accused him of not giving adequate attention to their project, and of re-thinking the details of a design while it was being built, and they were probably right. But the records also suggest that the authorities had no overall plan for the Castle, that they allowed it to grow without much thought for

the cost and that, for lack of County money, Harrison had sometimes had to spend his own to get work done at all. It is not surprising that relations became strained.

However, the Lancashire authorities were well pleased with their new Castle and in 1800 gave the fashionable London artist, Robert Freebairn, a £500 commission to paint a dozen very attractive watercolours of the project, which were presented to King George III, who was of course the Duke of Lancaster. Nine of them are used to illustrate this brief history. The external views suggest that building work was complete, but the interiors of the Crown Court and Shire Hall show little more than the structural shells without their proper

James Northcote's fine portrait of King George III, which has hung since 1800 in the Crown Court. (Lancaster Castle Project)

Freebairn's watercolour of the unfinished interior of the Crown Court. The wall on the right is the west wall of the Keep. (Lancaster City Museums)

fittings. The Shire Hall is a splendid ten-sided room, within whose walls a semi-circle of Gothic pillars carry not merely the arches which support the timber ceiling over the main part of the courtroom but also the arches of the plaster vault over the surrounding aisle; this is a most ingenious and beautiful solution, giving easy public access to the courtroom while allowing the business of the Court to proceed in suitably dignified surroundings.

More money became available after 1802 when the Treaty of Amiens brought a lull in the war with France. Joseph Gandy, a young architect who had been trained by James Wyatt and had worked for John Nash, was therefore called in to complete the furnishings and interior decoration of the Crown Court and Shire Hall. It was he who provided the designs for the window tracery, the seating and the elaborately detailed canopies over the judge's bench. One of Gandy's plans for the Shire Hall survives and is now in Sir John Soane's Museum in London. The earliest known illustration of the Shire Hall (painted in 1814) was acquired in 1993 for display to commemorate the thousand-year-long history of the Sheriffs—in some parts of England, if not in Lancashire. A more

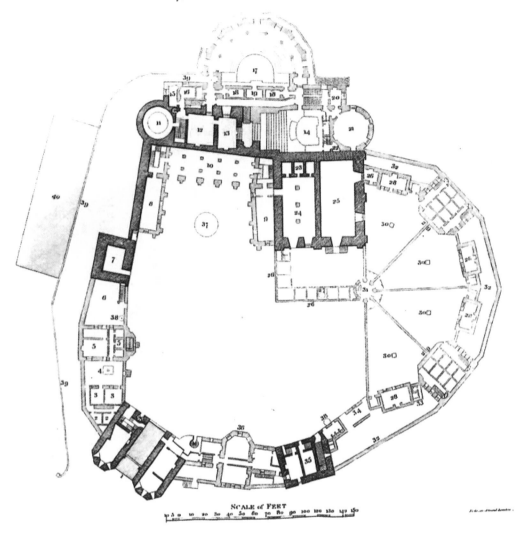

This plan of the Castle with most of the late 18th-century extensions was published in 1807, along with an enthusiastic description, in Christopher Clark's *Account of Lancaster*. Most of the buildings shown, except the dayrooms (no. 28), are there today, but the Dungeon Tower (7) was replaced in 1821 by the Female Penitentiary. Among the rooms which present-day visitors can see are Adrian's Tower (11), the Crown Court (14), the Shire Hall (17) and the Grand Jury Room (21). (Lancashire County Library)

interesting illustration of the Shire Hall in use for a trial in 1826 can be seen in the Barristers' Robing Room (and on page 33).

To put the finishing touch to the rebuilding of the Courts the portraits of the County Palatine's two Members of Parliament were hung in the Shire Hall, and a fine equestrian portrait of King George III was placed above the judge's bench in the Crown Court (see page 29). Behind the legs of the King's white horse (a symbol of Hanover where he was the Elector) one can see a view of the Castle and Priory Church from the north east, with Skerton Bridge in the foreground.

The last major extension to the Georgian County Gaol was the Female Penitentiary (10), which in 1821 replaced the medieval Dungeon Tower between the Gatehouse and

Freebairn's watercolour of the interior of the Shire Hall shows the structural shell before its fittings were installed to the design of Joseph Gandy in 1807. (Lancaster City Museums)

This watercolour, by an unknown artist, shows the trial in 1826 of Edward Gibbon Wakefield, who was accused of abducting the heiress of a rich Cheshire industrialist. He sits there, shamefaced, in the dock on the left. The standing barrister, who is pointing an accusing finger at him, is Henry Brougham, who later became Lord Chancellor and carried through a major programme of legal reforms in the 1830s. After serving his sentence, Wakefield played an important role in the 1830s and 1840s in the foundation of colonies in South Australia and New Zealand.
(Lancaster Castle Project)

Adrian's Tower. For this Gandy produced a design of considerable originality, based on Jeremy Bentham's ideas for the labour-saving supervision of prisoners. The building is semi-circular in plan and contains five tiers of cells, each with a window; these lead off curved internal galleries and are visible across an open space from a central control room. It is now the only building of its kind in existence.

Executions

CAPITAL PUNISHMENT was abolished in Britain in 1965, but two centuries ago death was the penalty for about two hundred serious crimes, which were known as felonies. Soon after the men's prison at Lancaster was complete, the Gaoler suggested that it would be more convenient if, after the Assizes, people convicted of a felony could be hanged in public near the Castle, rather than on the traditional site on the edge of the Moor (below the site of the present Ashton Memorial). The new round tower to the north of the courts was therefore altered in 1800, so that a door could open onto a specially constructed scaffold where the gallows were erected in what became known as Hanging Corner, opposite the churchyard. Until 1835 Lancaster was the home of the only Assize Courts in the whole of Lancashire, which then included the rapidly growing towns of Liverpool and Manchester; and so it is claimed that more people were sentenced to death here than in any other town in the kingdom.

Many felonies were crimes against property rather than against people, and in 1785 the Solicitor General admitted to Parliament that eighteen out of twenty people executed had committed a crime involving property worth less than a guinea—say, £150 in today's values— and that only one of the sixty-four people hanged

No picture exists of an execution at Hanging Corner. However, this watercolour sketch by the French artist, Théodore Géricault shows the members of the Cato Street Conspiracy (who had tried to organise the murder of the Cabinet in 1820) being prepared for their execution outside Newgate Prison in London. On the left the prison chaplain is trying to comfort one of the guilty men before he is blindfolded with a sort of hood. (Rouen, Musée des Beaux-Arts)

in England in the previous year had committed a murder. In consequence, many convicted felons were reprieved—282 out of 350 in 1805, for example—and in 1822 the number of crimes carrying the death penalty was halved.

Nevertheless, between 1782 and 1865 when Stephen Burke of Preston was 'turned off' for the murder of his wife, as many as 265 men and women were hanged at Lancaster. The County Executioner, 'Old Ned' Barlow, in a career spanning some thirty years, hanged 131 people, including nine on 19 April 1817, and Reverend Joseph Rowley, the prison chaplain between 1804 and 1858, attended no fewer than 168 executions.

It was hoped by the authorities that the public execution of a felon would be an edifying sight and would have a deterrent effect, and for this reason the boys of the local grammar school, where Joseph Rowley was a master for twenty-three years, were given a half-holiday. But for many Lancastrians 'hanging matches' were a very popular form of entertainment, watched by a crowd of thousands standing in the churchyard.

At the appointed time, the panelled door in the tower would open inwards, and the felons, accompanied by the chaplain and the hangman, would be led out, and their heads placed within the nooses. The implacable rigour of the process is nowhere better shown than by the upright wheelchair which can be seen in the Drop Room. This was made in 1828 for Jane Scott, who had murdered her mother, but was too weak to walk; the chair was therefore built to get her to the gallows in a standing position. If the felons were lucky,

The 'hanging chair' in which Jane Scott was brought to the scaffold in 1828. (Lancaster Castle Project)

they died instantly as their necks broke when they 'dropped'; otherwise it was a slow and public death by strangulation …

This licensed barbarity was stopped by the Private Executions Act of 1868, and after that time hangings took place in a building in the yard to the east of the Keep. The last hanging at Lancaster took place in 1910, but the 'topping shed' and 'drop' remained until 1965, when a change in the law made them finally redundant.

The setting of Freebairn's view of the Castle from the Moor was drawn with a degree of artistic licence in order to portray Lancaster and its Castle as picturesque places to visit on the way to the Lake District. (Lancaster City Museums)

The Castle in the Nineteenth Century

THE ONLY MAJOR ADDITION to the County Gaol in the nineteenth century was the low extension to one of the towers in the male felons' prison, which was built around 1850 following the pattern laid down at Pentonville Prison in London. Outside, this wing looks more forbidding than the older towers, because of its smaller windows, but it was perhaps more humane, since the windows gave light and air to the individual cells; the interior conforms to the now traditional stereotype of a prison, with long landings on either side of an open top-lit well.

This building is not shown on the large-scale Ordnance Survey map of Lancaster surveyed in 1845, but one which was so marked (though it had disappeared before a plan of the prison was drawn in 1877) is the treadwheel house. There were in fact two treadwheels in use at Lancaster for a number of years after 1822, primarily as a form of tiring punishment for prisoners sentenced to hard labour, but also to provide power for weaving looms or for pumps raising water from the Castle's wells.

One group of people, to whom reference has already been made, but who would not be found in prisons today, was debtors. When John Howard visited Lancaster in 1776, he found thirty-two of them, but when John Higgin retired as Keeper in 1833, there were frequently ten times as many. Debtors were not criminals, but merely people who could not pay their debts. They were often small businessmen or women with a temporary cash-flow problem. As long as they were in prison, their creditors could not obtain payment, but

This photograph, taken in 1858, must be the earliest one extant of Lancaster Castle, but it also shows Revd Joseph Rowley, Chaplain of the Gaol, in front of the Gatehouse—in his 86th year. (Lancashire County Library)

This (recently coloured) engraving by T. Allom shows the Arrival of the Judges at Lancaster Assizes in 1833—two years before the town lost its centuries-old monopoly of holding the major criminal trials in Lancashire. (Lancaster Tourism)

they could work at their trade or profession. A number of illustrations of the interior of the Castle in the eighteenth and nineteenth centuries (see pages 26 and 39) were drawn or even painted by debtor prisoners.

For those debtors who had no money life was very hard: they had to work around the prison and received a meagre daily ration of food. People in easy circumstances, however, had a relatively pleasant time—until 1869 when the Bankruptcy Act brought the system to an end. A prison inspector remarked in 1847 that the debtors' part of the Gaol 'resembled a somewhat noisy tavern or tea garden'. For this reason, perhaps, the Castle was sometimes known as 'Hansbrow's Hotel', after the name of the Governor between 1833 and 1862.

During the nineteenth century inspections of the County Gaols on behalf of the Home Office became more frequent—the first one at Lancaster was in 1812 and makes fascinating reading—and in 1835 the Home Office formed its Prison Inspectorate. After this the involvement of Sheriffs and JPs in the management of the County Gaol showed a marked decline. With the passing of the Prison Act of 1877 the County authorities gave up ownership and control of the prison to the Home Office, and the County Gaol was no more.

The Castle remained in use throughout the nineteenth century—as it remains today—as a court of law. The Quarter Sessions were held every three months to try minor offences, and also to provide some form of county-wide local government until the first Lancashire County Council was elected in 1889. And, of course, the Assizes were held twice a year to deal with more serious criminal cases.

Edward Slack was in prison for debt in the 1830s and made a number of sketches of the debtors' way of life, which were later engraved and published. This one shows a meal time in one of the better communal living rooms in the Keep. (Lancaster City Museums)

The Castle in the Twentieth Century

THE TWENTIETH CENTURY has not been without incidents. The last execution took place behind the Keep in 1910, and in 1916 the prison was closed, because a general reduction in the prison population made it surplus to the Home Office's requirements. An inspection by the Home Office in 1904 had already shown that it was no more than three-quarters full. For part of the First World War its cells were used for German prisoners, but thereafter the Home Office lent the Castle rent-free to the County Council. This seems to have caused some turmoil in Whitehall, for in 1924 the Treasury Solicitor gave his ruling that the Castle had always belonged to the King, and not to the County, let alone the Prison Commissioners. By 1931 the Home Office had acquiesced, and the Duchy of Lancaster granted a sixty-year lease of the Castle to the County Council, which used the former prison for training police cadets, until the new Police College was opened near Preston in 1937. The Courts were held, as always, in the buildings designed by Thomas Harrison.

The last course of policemen trained at Lancaster Castle, standing in front of the arcade of the Debtors' Wing at their passing-out parade in 1937. (Lancashire County Museums)

During the Second World War the Castle was occupied by the armed forces, and for a time housed the local control room of the Royal Observer Corps. From 1954 onwards the County Council has sub-let most of it again to the Home Office for use as a prison. Large-scale repairs were necessary in most buildings, and this work has continued until the present. In 1972 the Courts Act of 1971 came into effect: the twice yearly Assizes were abolished and the Crown Court was moved from Lancaster to Preston; but the Shire Hall and Crown Court are still in use as a third-tier court trying less serious cases. Since it is linked internally to the prison, this Court has also been used for a number of high-security trials—even though this causes problems for the normal running of the prison, which is not a high-security establishment.

Hopes that the prison would close in time for some of the Castle to be opened in a limited way to the public in 1993 to celebrate the 900th anniversary of its foundation by Roger of Poitou have not been fulfilled, but what is called the Lancaster Castle Project has been established by Lancashire County Council, in co-operation with Lancaster City Council and the Duchy of Lancaster. It has commissioned the Lancaster University Archaeological Unit to carry out a long-term survey of all the buildings of the Castle, in the hope that some of the many questions about the medieval Castle may be answered. Its eventual aim is, however, to give public access to the main courtyard and then to develop the Castle as a major tourist attraction, as soon as the prison does close—perhaps in 1996.

Freebairn's south-west view of the Castle is—like the one from the Moor on page 36— drawn with some artistic licence to give a Romantic grandeur to the scenery, but the essence of the view from Aldcliffe is unchanged today. (Lancaster City Museums)

The County Palatine and Duchy of Lancaster

LANCASHIRE'S TRADITIONAL NAME is the County Palatine of Lancaster, and yet the Queen is the Duke of Lancaster and enjoys the revenues of the Duchy. This slightly confusing wealth of titles does, however, have a straightforward explanation, and a brief look at the holders of the Honour of Lancaster in the later Middle Ages will help to explain it.

The story starts when Henry III granted the Honour of Lancaster to his youngest son Edmund Crouchback in 1267. Edmund already held extensive estates in Wales and the East Midlands, but he came to live mainly at Lancaster and called himself the Earl of Lancaster. He supported his elder brother Edward I during the wars of conquest in Wales and Scotland, but his son Thomas, the second Earl, was more critical of Edward II and paid for his 'disloyalty' with his life.

Earl Thomas' younger brother, Henry, was, however, among the barons who conspired to depose Edward II in 1327, and so a grateful Edward III restored to him his late brother's title and lands. Henry died in 1345 and was followed, as the fourth Earl, by his son, who was also called Henry. Since both of them, father and son, had been loyal in their service to him, Edward III rewarded the fourth Earl in 1351 by creating him Duke of Lancaster.

Instead of marking this honour by granting Duke Henry more lands, Edward III gave him the privilege of holding what were called 'palatine powers' in Lancashire during his lifetime. This meant that he had almost royal authority within the County (which became a County Palatine) and thus a larger income. When he was Earl, his income had come from his extensive estates and from the profits of dispensing justice in the local Courts which he controlled; now that he was Duke with palatine powers, he could also keep the fees which he obtained from the administration of justice in the serious criminal cases tried at the Lancaster Assizes.

Duke Henry died in 1361, and with him the Dukedom and the palatine powers. He had had no sons, but his daughter, Blanche, had previously married Edward III's

This picture of John of Gaunt—an idealised image of a royal Duke—was copied in 1792 from a stained glass window, made in 1440 and now in the Antechapel of All Souls' College, Oxford.
(Lancaster City Museums)

fourth son, John of Gaunt. She therefore brought to her husband the Lancaster estates which had been held by her father, and this made John of Gaunt such a wealthy man that Edward III gave him the title of Duke of Lancaster in 1362. It was not, however, until he was on his death-bed in 1377 that the King also gave John of Gaunt palatine powers. Though loyal to the next King, his nephew, Richard II, John of Gaunt was also ambitious and in 1390 persuaded Richard to confirm that the Dukedom and palatine powers should descend to his heirs—which made him virtually King in Lancashire.

Richard II, like Edward II, took more interest in the arts than in politics and warfare. John of Gaunt's eldest son, Henry of Bolingbroke, was more critical of the King than was his father and he was banished in 1398. On the death of John of Gaunt in 1399, Richard exiled Henry for life and confiscated his Duchy lands and titles—a high-handed action which alarmed many of his barons. Henry invaded Yorkshire with a handful of men in July 1399 and swore an oath that he sought no more than his rights. This won him the support of many northern barons, so the King decided to negotiate, but Henry took him prisoner and transferred him to the Tower of London. Despite his oath he persuaded the King to

abdicate in September and then prevailed on Parliament to acknowledge him as King Henry IV. Within a couple of months Richard had died in Henry's castle at Pontefract.

From 1399 onwards, therefore, the Duchy lands (which included many estates outside Lancashire) have always belonged to the reigning King or Queen. When Henry Duke of Lancaster became King, having returned to England with the primary objective of reclaiming his Duchy, he immediately decreed that his Duchy inheritance should be held separate from the other Crown lands, and administered by a Duchy Council. Although it was his intention that the Duchy lands should pass to his heirs (whether they were Kings of England or not) it was established by charter in 1461 that the Duchy should be recognized and incorporated as a separate inheritance, held for the Kings and Queens of England for ever. Thus the Chancellor of the Duchy of Lancaster (who originally sat as the judge in the Duchy's Courts) became the officer responsible to the Sovereign for the administration of his or her Duchy. Although his post, through the evolution of a parliamentary form of government, has now become one of the Offices of State, the Chancellor remains responsible to the Sovereign personally for the Duchy of Lancaster's affairs.

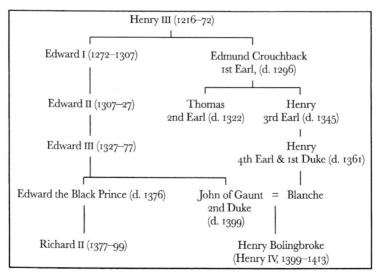

This family tree shows that the Earls and Dukes of Lancaster were close relatives of the Plantagenet Kings of England.